W9-APD-361

For Mom With Love

Copyright © 1987, 1994
Brownlow Publishing Company
6309 Airport Freeway
Fort Worth, Texas 76117

All rights reserved. The use or reprinting of any part
of this book without the express written permission
of the publisher is prohibited.

Page 28: "A Mom's Life," from *Funny Sauce* by Delia Ephron.

Every effort has been made to contact the various authors
of writings in this book; however, some could not be located
and are unknown to the writer and publisher. Questions in
this regard should be directed to the publisher.

All writing in this book not otherwise attributed
is by the author.

Cover/Interior/Illustration:
Koechel Peterson & Associates

Printed in the United States of America.

ISBN 0-915720-68-X

10 9 8

A Special Gift

For:

_____

From:

_____

Date:

_____

For Mom With Love

Written and Compiled by

MARY HOLLINGSWORTH

Brownlow Gift Books

A Psalm in My Heart
Angels of Mercy, Whispers of Love
Cheerful Hearts
Flowers for Mother
Flowers for You
Flowers of Friendship
Flowers That Never Fade
For Mom With Love
Give Us This Day
Grandpa Was a Preacher
Jesus Wept
Leaves of Gold
Let's Laugh a Little
Making the Most of Life
Thoughts of Gold—Wisdom for Living
Today and Forever
Today Is Mine
University of Hard Knocks

To my
own sweet mom,
Thelma Shrode,
with love

"*Her children arise
and call her blessed;
her husband also,
and he praises her.*"

(Proverbs 31:28)

A mother is someone
who dreams great dreams
for you, but then
she lets you chase
the dreams you
have for yourself and
loves you just the same.

I Remind Myself of You

Sometimes at the most unlikely moments I remind myself of you, Mom. And it may be the way I move my hand, or the freckles on my arms. Sometimes it's something I say that sounds like you would say it. And I catch myself arranging my kitchen the way you always do, because it just seems right somehow. I only know how to make one kind of stew—the kind you always make—and it almost seems irreverent to add anything to it or leave anything out.

Sometimes I remind myself of you. And that's just fine, because I'd like nothing better than to be like you. But I wonder...do you ever remind yourself of me?

The Mother of Inventions

It had been a long week. Creating things was tiring. In fact, he had stopped to rest a whole day before he continued. That last creature, the one he called "man," had really been tricky. He never did get everything into that one that he had intended to. There were a lot of parts left over that simply wouldn't fit into one unit. It became too complex.

He sighed. He really did want to make a creation in his own image, but maybe that was asking too much. Then he had an idea. Quickly he reviewed the schematic and the drawings of the first creation. Yes! That was it. So, he gently removed one of the parts from the man, picked up all the leftover parts and went to his workshop. There he laid out all the parts and did a mental inventory. Whew! This was still going to be difficult. But he started to work anyway.

It was a long time later when the Lord looked up from his work, stretched his aching back and rubbed

his tired eyes. Then a little smile started to creep across his lips. As he carefully examined the finished creation, he began to laugh with delight. "I'm brilliant," he said. And all of the angels in the workshop agreed.

"Look at this," he said excitedly, and the angels gathered around. He pointed out the soft shoulders, the strong back, the extra eyes and hands. He showed them the sturdy springs in the legs, the padded feet and the knee pads. Then he let them examine the engine. It was a complicated system, run by a tough but flexible little heart. And finally he showed them the safety valve that let hot, salty water trickle out through some tiny holes in the corners of the eyes when too much pressure built up inside.

"Fascinating," said one of the angels.

"Yes," said the Lord, "but you haven't seen the best part yet." Then he lifted the lid of the creature and showed them a tiny computer.

"What does that do?" asked a tiny angel on his right.

"This is the most remarkable invention I've ever made," said the Lord proudly. "It works almost exactly like my own mind. It can turn sadness into joy, strife into peace and despair into hope. It can convert hatred into love and failure into success. And it has an incredible little merge-purge device that

A mother

is the one

through whom God

whispers love

to his little children.

allows it to combine all its good experiences and eliminate all its evil files until its memory storage is practically pure and accurate. And it comes complete with a whole raft of software packages."

"What do you mean?" asked an inquisitive angel.

"Well, it can be programmed to act in a wide variety of ways. It can be a financial analyst to evaluate household budgets, a word processor to take care of family business correspondence or a giant flow chart and calendar to keep track of activities for a family of eight. It can become a scorekeeper for everything from little league baseball to how well the stocks are doing on Wall Street. But it also has creative packages such as graphics for grade school art projects, music writing abilities for graduated levels of piano recitals and a craft software that will construct marvelous science projects out of household scraps. It has a preprogrammed package of the complete works of Betty Crocker, a do-it-yourself-repair-anything manual and Hoyle's book of rules for every game ever known."

"Wow! I've never seen anything like it before," said one amazed angel. "What are you going to call it?"

"Oh, that's the easy part. There's only one word that adequately describes it," said the Lord. "I'm going to call it 'Mother.'"

A mother

is God's love

in action.

A Million Little Things

hanks, Mom, not only for the many big things you've done for me through the years, but also for the million little things you've done.

Oh, I know you didn't think I was keeping count, but I remember how many times you combed my hair, made popcorn while the rest of us watched TV, ironed my favorite blouse for school the next day, listened to me practice the same old boogie on the piano, fed the dog when I forgot, made banana nut cake because it's my favorite, went without a dress so I could have one, fixed my lunch for school and drove me to play practice.

I remember the dishes you washed, the permanents you gave, the cookies you baked, the rips you repaired and the slumber parties you gave. I remember the picnics we had, the times you played Tooth Fairy and Santa Claus and the

Easter Bunny, the birthday parties you gave and the books you read to me over and over again.

On second thought, maybe it wasn't a million—maybe it was more like a zillion or something! But who's counting?

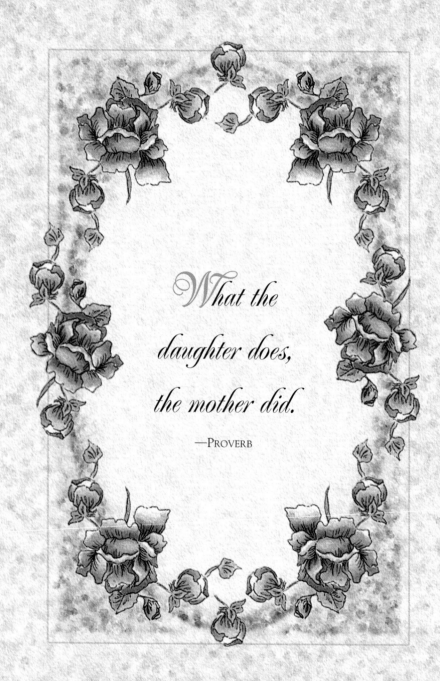

What the daughter does, the mother did.

—PROVERB

We leave

traces of ourselves

wherever we go,

on whatever

we touch.

—LEWIS THOMAS

A Miracle

A mother is not a person; she's a miracle. She can turn into anything she needs to be in an instant. She's like the star of a science fiction movie who drinks a magic potion and transforms into marvelous, superhuman creatures. She can turn into a nurse, just at the sight of a scrape or scratch. And at the wave of a wand, she appears as Cinderella ready for the ball. When trouble threatens, she becomes a mighty fortress behind which the whole family huddles for protection—even Dad. Or she "wiggles her nose" and becomes a little league coach, a Girl Scout leader, a homeroom mother, a Sunday school teacher, a play director, a counselor, a playmate or a volunteer for Jerry's kids. She can be a cook, a maid, a taxi driver and a referee all in the space of a few minutes. She can turn into a shrewd merchant at a garage sale, an orator at PTA, an enchanting storyteller at the day care center and a military genius in organizing the neighborhood against crime. Oh, there's no question about it—she's not a person; she's a miracle!

A mother

is the one

who is still

there when

everyone else

has deserted you.

New Mother

"I will let nothing hurt you,"
She told the child asleep;
And wept because the promise
Was one she could not keep.

"But I will never hurt you,"
She said again and wept,
Knowing it a promise
No mortal ever kept.

"Life has deep hurts," she whispered,
"Which no one can avert.
God help me teach you strength and love
For conquering any hurt."

—Jane Merchant - *In Green Pastures*

*God pardons
like a mother, who
kisses the offense into
everlasting forgetfulness.*

—Unknown

A

mother's children

are portraits

of herself.

—Unknown

Loving ways

just seem

to come naturally

to you, Mom.

Mender

A mother is a mender. She mends socks, clothes and broken dolls. She mends furniture, clocks and venetian blinds. Sometimes she fixes broken bike chains and other things that "come loose" in life. But most often she mends a child's broken heart or a daddy's broken spirit. She puts crushed feelings back together again and glues them tight with a drop of super-love. Sometimes she mends a little bird's broken wing or removes a grass burr from a puppy's foot. She is, in her own gentle way, a minister of mending, and she takes her ministry very seriously. She goes about her mending with words of kindness, acts of love and the healing balm of compassion. She's a mender because she's a mother.

You're

more than

just a mom—

you're one

of my

best friends.

A Mom's Life

Take your plate into the kitchen, please.
Take it downstairs when you go.
Don't leave it there, take it upstairs.
Is that yours?
Don't hit your brother.
I'm talking to you.
Just a minute, please, can't you see
    I'm talking?
I said, don't interrupt.
Did you brush your teeth?
What are you doing out of bed?
Go back to bed.
You can't watch in the afternoon.
What do you mean, there's nothing to do?
Go outside.
Read a book.
Turn it down.
Get off the phone.
Tell your friend, you'll call her back.
    Right now!
Hello. No, she's not home.
She's still not home.

She'll call you when she gets home.
Take a jacket. Take a sweater.
Take one, anyway.
Someone left his shoes in front of the TV.
Get the toys out of the hall. Get the toys out
    of the bathtub. Get the toys off the stairs.
Do you realize that could kill someone?
Hurry up.
Hurry up. Everyone's waiting.
I'll count to ten and then we're going
    without you.
Did you go to the bathroom?
If you don't go, you're not going.
I mean it.
Why didn't you go before you left?
Can you hold it?
What's going on back there?
Stop it.
I said, stop it!
I don't want to hear about it.
Stop it, or I'm taking you home right now.
That's it. We're going home.
Give me a kiss.
I need a hug.

To love
and be loved
is like
being warmed
by the sun
from both sides
at once.

—Unknown

Make your bed.
Clean up your room.
Set the table.
I need you to set the table!
Don't tell me it's not your turn.
Please move your chair into the table.
Sit up.
Just try a little. You don't have to eat
    the whole thing.
Stop playing and eat.
Would you watch what you're doing?
Move your glass, it's too close to the edge.
Watch it!
More, what?
More, *please*. That's better.
Just eat one bite of salad.
You don't always get what you want. That's life.
Don't argue with me. I'm not
    discussing this anymore.
Go to your room.
No, ten minutes are not up.
One more minute.
How many times have I told you,
    don't do that.

Where did the cookies go?
Eat the old fruit before you eat the new fruit.
I'm not giving you mushrooms. I've taken all
    the mushrooms out.
      See.
Is your homework done?
Stop yelling. If you want to ask me something,
    come here.
Stop yelling. If you want to ask me something,
    come here.
I'll think about it.
Not now.
Ask your father.
We'll see.
Don't sit so close to the television,
    it's bad for your eyes.
Calm down.
Calm down and start over.
Is that the truth?
Fasten your seat belt.
Did everyone fasten their seat belts?
I'm sorry, that's the rule. I'm sorry, that's
    the rule. I'm sorry, that's the rule.

—Delia Ephron

The Heart
of Christmas

The heart of Christmas can't be found

In trees that glimmer light

Or fancy presents tied around

With ribbon glistening bright.

It can't be found in Santa's face

Or sleigh bells from above…

The gentle heart of Christmas

Is my mother's special love.

Your mother's quiet smile

is like an a cappella sunrise

in your heart.

A Collage of Home

Popcorn. Dad reading the Bible. Hot apple cider. A fire in the fireplace with Christmas stockings hung all around. The cat curled up on the rug. Dominoe parties. Grandpa's old library table in the corner. The aroma of bacon cooking early in the morning. Quilting frames and the Singer sewing machine. Having to be extra quiet on Sunday morning so Dad could study his Sunday school lesson. Putting together jigsaw puzzles on a cold day. The old striking clock on the hall. The squeaking rocker in the den. Saturday night TV. Warm, homemade bread with butter. Making doll clothes. Picking out pecans on the halves—saving half and eating half. Singing and telling jokes with my brother. The Sunday color comics. Mom.

Teacher

You taught me a lot of things, Mom—more than any other teacher. You taught me how to cook and sew, how to dust and clean and do the laundry. You taught me how to shop for groceries and compare prices, how to plant flowers and even how to "play second fiddle." And you never got angry when I learned slowly or made mistakes. You just patiently started again and again until I could do it on my own.

But you also taught me the more important things in life—things that made life exciting and worthwhile. You taught me it was more blessed to give than to receive by taking cakes to the neighbors. You taught me to love the lonely by visiting the retirement homes and your aging relatives and friends. You taught me the meaning of humility by quietly serving others and taking no credit for yourself. And you taught me kindness by the way you spoke to the mailman, the paperboy and the old man who came to our back door for something to eat. You taught me how to live.

A mom's gift

is always the best

because it's wrapped

in love and tied up

with heartstrings.

The father

is the head

of the home,

but the mother is

the heart of the home.

Someday

omeday when the kids are grown, life will be different. The memo pad on my refrigerator will read, "Afternoon at hairdresser," or, "Browse through art gallery," or "Start golf lessons," instead of "Pediatrician at 2:00," "Cub Pack Meeting at 4:00."

Someday, when the kids are grown, the house will be free of graffiti. There will be no crayoned smiley faces on walls, no names scrawled in furniture dust, no pictures fingered on steamy windows, and no initials etched in bars of soap.

Someday, when the kids are grown, I'll get through a whole chapter of an engrossing book without being interrupted to sew a nose on a teddy bear, stop a toddler from eating the dog food, or rescue the cat from the toy box.

Someday, when the kids are grown, I won't find brown apple cores under the beds, empty spindles on the toilet paper hanger, or fuzzy caterpillars in

denim jeans. And I will be able to find a pencil in the desk drawer, a slice of leftover pie in the refrigerator, and the comics still in the center of the newspaper.

Someday, when the kids are grown, I'll breeze right past the gumball machine in the supermarket without having to fumble for pennies; I'll stroll freely down each aisle without fear of inadvertently passing the candy or toy sections; and I'll choose cereal without considering what noise it makes, what prize it contains, or what color it comes in.

Someday, when the kids are grown, I'll prepare quiche Lorraine, or scallops amandine, or just plain liver and onions, and no one will say, "Yuk! I wish we were having hot dogs!" or, "Jimmy's lucky—his mom lets him eat chocolate bars for dinner." And we'll eat by candlelight, with no one trying to roast their peas and carrots over the flame to "make them taste better," or arguing about who gets to blow out the candle when we're done.

Houses

are made of

wood and stone,

but only love

can make a home.

Someday, when the kids are grown, I'll get ready for my bath without first having to remove a fleet of boats, two rubber alligators, and a soggy tennis ball from the tub. I'll luxuriate in hot, steamy water and billows of bubbles for a whole hour, and no fist will pound on the door—no small voices will yell, "Hurry up, Mommy. I gotta go!"

Yes, someday when the kids are grown, life will be different. They'll leave our nest, and the house will be
Quiet...
　　and Calm...
　　　　and Empty...
　　　　　　and Lonely...
　　　　　　　　And I won't like that
　　　　　　　　　　at all.

And then I'll spend my time, not looking forward to *Someday*, but looking back at *Yesterday*.

—SANDI FRANKLIN

$\mathcal{B}e$ it
ever so humble,
there's no place
like home.

Chubby Hands

Her chubby hands
crept round my neck
And whispered words
I can't forget.
They cast a light
upon my soul—
On secrets no one knew.
They startled me,
I hear them yet:
"Someday I'll be like you!"

—Unknown

Rejecting things because they are old-fashioned would rule out the sun and the moon— and a mother's love.

—Anonymous

Improvising

I look back now, Mom, and I'm amazed at your resourcefulness. At the time, it seemed so easy for you, but now I know that it was sacrifice and creativity in their purest forms. When I refused to eat anything except apple pie, you made "apple" pie from pears (because that's all we had), used plenty of cinnamon and sugar, and I never knew the difference. (That may have been the best apple pie you ever made.)

When I would only drink "store-bought" milk, and we didn't have the time or money to go to the store, you mixed up powdered milk, poured it into the empty milk carton from the store and put it in the refrigerator. It was delicious, just like "store-bought" milk ought to be. When I wanted a new coat—something fancy that no one else had—you made me a colorful Joseph's jacket out of scraps of leftover material. I still think it was one of the fanciest coats I ever had. All my friends were jealous.

I was a lucky kid because I had you for a mom.
I learned creativity and resourcefulness, but most
of all I learned to believe in sacrificing...
improvising...and loving.

A

mother's love is

not blind; it's

just very nearsighted.

My mother is

too kind in what she

says about me; her

affection blinds

her a little.

Mom,

thanks for always

seeing the

best in me,

even if sometimes

you have to

strain

to see it.

Non-Working Mother

I don't know who coined the phrase "non-working mother," but whoever it was didn't know my mother. He didn't watch the sweat run down her face as she scrubbed and waxed hardwood floors. He didn't see her soak her tired and aching feet after a whole day of walking alongside the junior high band in the Thanksgiving parade. He was never there to see her collapsed in the old recliner after mowing, raking, edging and cleaning up the entire yard by herself in the August heat because Dad had to go to the office. He didn't see her doze off in front of the TV because she was so worn out from a day of spring cleaning. He wasn't there to help when the house had to be repainted or rooms had to be re-wallpapered. And he evidently never watched her pack and unpack, load and unload the entire household when we moved. Most folks couldn't survive such a leisurely, non-working life of luxury, I think.

There is

no such thing as a

non-working mother.

—HESTER MUNDIS

Happy Birthday to You

I always have the strangest sensation on my birthday that you're being overlooked. I feel as if I should send you flowers or bake you a cake on the anniversary of the day you gave birth to me. After all, it was your birthday, too. And you did all the work. I just showed up at the last minute to grab all the glory. Everybody "oood" and "ahhhd" over me, but they should have been in awe of you. Candles should be lit in your honor, not mine. And you're the one who should get the presents— you deserve them after all you went through. Well, I guess it's just not meant to be that way. Oh, don't get me wrong; I like to celebrate my birthday. But just between you and me, Mom, I know I couldn't have done it without you.

I could

never find a more

wonderful mom,

even if I went to

the end of

a rainbow.

Handmade

others can't be stereotyped. They're not perfect angels cut out with God's cookie cutter. Each one is unique, special and handmade. Mothers come in all shapes and sizes, dressed in anything from frilly frocks to denim jeans, managing everything from tiny households to giant corporations. She can be anything from a preacher's wife to a plumber. But she is her children's source of life and love and security, no matter how she looks or acts or seems to others. She's "Mother," and that fact alone covers a multitude of imperfections and inadequacies. After all, Mama doesn't have to be perfect; she only has to be here when I need her.

The best thing mothers can spend on their children is time, not money.

—ANONYMOUS

Whenever I want to feel

especially good about myself,

I just remember that

I have you for a mom.

A Mother Is

A mother is not a person to lean on but a person to make leaning unnecessary.

—Dorothy Fischer

All mothers are physically handicapped.
They have only two hands.

—Anonymous

Judicious mothers will always keep in mind that they are the first book read, and the last put aside, in every child's library.

—C. Lenox Remond

A mother should be like a quilt—keep the children warm but don't smother them.

—Anonymous

A mother is a mother still
The holiest thing alive.

—Samuel Taylor Coleridge

I Took His Hand and Followed

My dishes went unwashed today,
I didn't make the bed.
I took his hand and followed
where his eager footsteps led.

Oh, yes, we went adventuring,
my little son and I...
Exploring all the great outdoors
beneath the summer sky.

We waded in a crystal stream,
we wandered through a wood...
My kitchen wasn't swept today,
but life was rich and good.

We found a cool, sun-dappled glade,
and now my small son knows
How mother bunny hides her nest,
where jack-in-the-pulpit grows.

We watched a robin feed her young,
   we climbed a sunlit hill...
Saw cloud-sheep scamper through the sky,
   we plucked a daffodil.

That my house was neglected,
   that I didn't brush the stairs,
In twenty years no one on earth will know
   or even care.

But that I've helped my little boy
   to noble manhood grow
In twenty years the whole wide world
   may look and see and know.

—Unknown

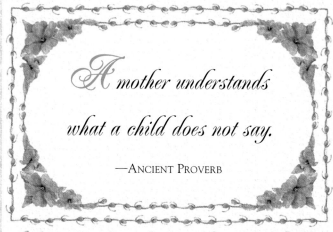

A mother understands

what a child does not say.

—ANCIENT PROVERB

Just as I Am

It's always so relaxing to come home where I can just be myself. Nobody cares if I have a hole in my sock or if I stay in my house shoes all day long. I don't have to pretend to be anybody or anything but me, and what a relief that is compared to the daily rat race I face. Mom wouldn't even care if I brought my dirty laundry home with me to do. She likes me, dirty laundry and all. She knows I'm no genius, and that's okay. But she believes in me and thinks I can do great things anyway, and that's nice. I'm glad there's at least one person in the world who knows all about me and still loves me.

Mom, thanks for loving me just as I am.

Hold Me, Mama

I'm not a little child anymore, but sometimes I wish I were. Life was better then. I could make a Slo-Poke sucker last all day long and jump double-rope for 15 minutes without getting out of breath. When we played Jacks I could do pigs-in-a-pen all the way up to twelves. And I was the grand-slam champion in YMCA baseball. Every Sunday night my dad took us to the Dairy Queen for ice cream, and I could blow bubblegum bubbles bigger than any other kid on our block. A Coke was a real treat with a bag of peanuts with it, and saddle oxfords were not only sturdy, but stylish. Life was better then because, when I got hurt, I could run home to my mom. She'd kiss away my tears, put a Band-Aid on my knee, then take me into her lap and rock me until the pain went away or I fell asleep. Sometimes when life is rough I'd just like to be a kid again so I could say, "Hold me, Mama."

Thanks

for listening,

Mom.

Mom,

I hope you know

that I love you.